Queen Elizabeth II

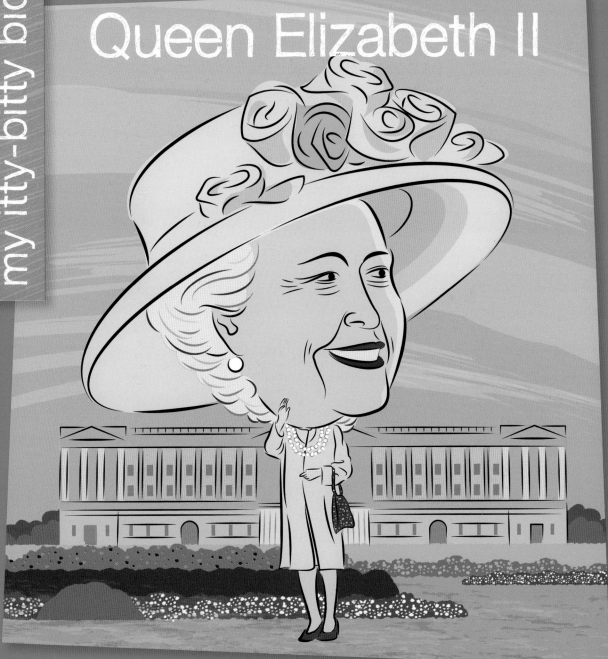

![Cherry Lake Press logo] CHERRY LAKE PRESS

Published in the United States of America by Cherry Lake Publishing Group
Ann Arbor, Michigan
www.cherrylakepublishing.com

Reading Adviser: Beth Walker Gambro, MS, Ed., Reading Consultant, Yorkville, IL
Book Designer: Jennifer Wahi
Illustrator: Jeff Bane

Photo Credits: Photo Credits: page 5: © Classic Image/Alamy Stock Photo; page 7: © World History Archive/Alamy Stock Photo; page 9: © Everett Collection/Alamy Stock Photo; pages 11, 22: © Mirrorpix/Alamy Stock Photo; page 13: © Pictorial Press/Alamy Stock Photo; pages 15, 23: © Krakenimages.com/Shutterstock; page 17: © Lorna Roberts/Shutterstock; page 19: © Jack Hill/The Times/Alamy Stock Photo; page 21: © Rebecca Naden/Alamy Stock Photo

Cherry Lake Press is an imprint of Cherry Lake Publishing Group.

Names: Gebhardt, Amanda, author. | Bane, Jeff, 1957- illustrator.
Title: Queen Elizabeth II / written by: Amanda Gebhardt ; illustrated by: Jeff Bane.
Other titles: Queen Elizabeth the Second
Description: Ann Arbor, Michigan : Cherry Lake Publishing, [2023] | Series: My itty-bitty bio | Includes index. | Audience: Grades K-1 | Summary: "This biography for early readers examines the life of Queen Elizabeth II, the former queen of England, in a simple, age-appropriate way that helps young readers develop word recognition and reading skills. Includes table of contents, author biography, timeline, glossary, index, and other informative backmatter. The My Itty-Bitty Bio series celebrates diversity, covering women and men from a range of backgrounds and professions including immigrants and individuals with disabilities"-- Provided by publisher.
Identifiers: LCCN 2022044022 | ISBN 9781668918456 (hardcover) | ISBN 9781668926338 (paperback) | ISBN 9781668926345 (ebook) | ISBN 9781668926352 (pdf)
Subjects: LCSH: Elizabeth II, Queen of Great Britain, 1926-2022--Juvenile literature. | Queens--Great Britain--Biography--Juvenile literature.
Classification: LCC DA590 .G43 2023 | DDC 941.085092 [B]--dc23/eng/20220915
LC record available at https://lccn.loc.gov/2022044022

Printed in the United States of America
Corporate Graphics

table of contents

My Story .4

Timeline. .22

Glossary 24

Index 24

About the author: Amanda Gebhardt is a writer, editor, and life-long learner. She lives in Ann Arbor, Michigan, with her husband, two kids, and one playful pup named Cookie.

About the illustrator: Jeff Bane and his two business partners own a studio along the American River in Folsom, California, home of the 1849 Gold Rush. When Jeff's not sketching or illustrating for clients, he's either swimming or kayaking in the river to relax.

I was born in London in 1926.
My grandfather was a **king**.

I was a princess. My family called me Lilibet. I called my grandpa Grandpa England.

What does your family call you?

I had a little sister. Her name was Margaret. She was a princess, too.

Do you have a brother or a sister?

My dad became king. Our country went to war. I served my country. I was a driver and **mechanic**.

How do you help other people?

I met my husband when I was young. We wrote each other letters. We got married. We had four children.

I became **Queen** of the United Kingdom. They put my picture on money.

The world changed a lot. My children grew up. Their children grew up. I was a great-grandmother.

I lived in Buckingham Palace. I met world **leaders**. I gave important speeches.

The country celebrated my **reign** in 2022. I died later that year. I had been queen for 70 years.

What would you like to ask me?

1945

1920

Born
1926

1952

2020

↑
Died
2022

glossary

king (KING) a male ruler

leaders (LEE-ders) people who help make rules and laws

mechanic (muh-KAN-ik) a person who repairs machines such as cars and trucks

queen (KWEEN) a female ruler

reign (RAYN) the time a king or queen rules

index

birth, 4, 22
Buckingham Palace, 18

death, 23

family, 4, 6–10, 12–13, 16–17

kings, 4, 6, 10

London, England, 4, 18

Margaret, Princess, 8–9
marriage, 12–13
mechanics, 10, 11
money, 14–15

Philip, Prince, 12, 13, 17
princesses, 6, 8, 9

queens, 14–21

reign, 20

timeline, 22–23

world leaders, 18–19
World War II, 10–11

Children's BIO

Gebhardt, Amanda
Queen Elizabeth II

03/30/23